Tree-Lined Streets of Queens

poems by

James McKee

Finishing Line Press
Georgetown, Kentucky

Tree-Lined Streets of Queens

*To my wife, Annie,
who saw what I could not*

Copyright © 2025 by James McKee
ISBN 979-8-89990-191-1 First Edition
All rights reserved under International and Pan-American Copyright Conventions. No part of this book may be reproduced in any manner whatsoever without written permission from the publisher, except in the case of brief quotations embodied in critical articles and reviews.

ACKNOWLEDGMENTS

My thanks to the editors of the following journals, in which these poems (or earlier versions of them) first appeared: *The Arlington Literary Journal; The Banyan Review; Beltway Poetry Quarterly; Burningword Literary Journal; Cottonwood; The Dalhousie Review; Eclectica; Fourteen Hills; Grist; The Macguffin; The Main Street Rag; Mudlark; Newtown Literary; New World Writing; New York Quarterly; Nine Cloud Journal; The Ocotillo Review; Pine Row; Roanoke Review; The Sandy River Review; Southern Poetry Review; Tiny Seed Literary Journal; Vallum; Vita Brevis Poetry Magazine; The Writing Disorder*

I would like to thank Christen Kincaid, my editor at Finishing Line Press, for all her work on TLSQ.

Publisher: Leah Huete de Maines
Editor: Christen Kincaid
Cover Art and Design: James McKee
Author Photo: James McKee

Order online: www.finishinglinepress.com
also available on amazon.com

Author inquiries and mail orders:
Finishing Line Press
PO Box 1626
Georgetown, Kentucky 40324
USA

Contents

I
Protocol for Meet-ups in the Park	1
The Fallacy of Composition	2
Synchronicity	3
What's Not to Like?	5
A Visit from the E-Muse	6
Confessional	8
Bequest	10

II
Making It Up: An Elegy	17

III
Off into the Sunset	25
East River Suite	27
Poem about Love (Not a Love Poem)	30
By Sapphire Pool, Yellowstone	32
A Brief Loss of Momentum	33
A Long Walk on an Empty Beach	34
On Being Deciduous	36
Víti, a Volcanic Lake in Iceland	37
Black Beach Idyll	38
Autumn Exit	39
The View from Land's End	40
NaCl	43
All or Nothing/Nothing at All	44

IV
Another CNN-Induced Lyric Outburst	47
"I Did It Because I Am Free"	48
White Lies	50
Sound Effect	52
Field-Notes from Monster Season	54
Scrolling through Weimar	58
Staying Sharp	59
Premonitions of Civil War	61
Terminus	62

NOTES	63

What kind of times are they, when
A talk about trees is almost a crime
Because it implies silence about so many horrors?

                Bertold Brecht

[. . .] why do I tell you
anything? Because you still listen, because in times like these
to have you listen at all, it's necessary
to talk about trees.

                Adrienne Rich

I

Protocol for Meet-ups in the Park

You're not combing these paths for yet more proofs
of a rupture far beyond repair.
Floods keep shifting the statues. Droughts.
It's not like more tulips would matter.

You know better than to want consoling, which is good,
given this crime scene they call a lawn.
And you're sick of nice-nice distractions, even if
among ducks and such, they still happen.

Because it's the trees that bring you here. Me too.
A hot wind sluices them like an unseen river.
With us, complicity's just old news.
The figures their tossing leaves trace, never.

The Fallacy of Composition

Mapped onscreen,
the city redresses
its ragged edges
with street-grid filigree
and suturing bridges.
As if checked mid-jostle,
its digitized islands
practically nestle.
Awkward curlicues
of cerulean water
caulk them together
like the rowdiest tiles,
aswim in cement
and bench-embedded,
from a whimsy of Gaudi's.

But absent that device,
the estuary's expanse
unspools otherwise.
Splinters of land
limn impact zones
as if something steel
struck something stone.
Though it's ages since
both ocean and river
flooded in like lymph
to a limb just injured,
puckering as from
an ill-healed wound
still buckles beneath
the avenues' weave.

Always the same mistake.
Not that everything breaks—
got it, thanks—
but how contriving
a whole from its parts
requires disguising
the woes that made,
and make, them sharp.

Synchronicity

> *"the meaningful coincidence of two or more events where something other than the probability of chance is involved"*
>
> Jung

It's the cut that does it: abrupt, but too clean
to seem cruel. One look and I know, as if
some rando with *ta-da!* on his breath is murmuring
Behold, the way the Spirit of Christmas Past
ambushes Scrooge with his fresh young self. But hold on,
let's back up.
          Not far from where I write, plane trees
portico a street like years of a life, dwindling
each way. I'd walked there often enough to confuse
routine with knowledge, till one day the wisps
of elapsed decades condensed into an emblem
whose uncanny gravity still grapples me
whenever I pass.
          Pegging the nth plane's foot
is the stump of an outgrown prop, a pole sawn flush
to the roots it once buttressed against whatever
could blight a sapling's skyward climb. It'd stood
over their tendrils long enough to be clutched
like a rung, until the day somebody wise,
or kind, or maybe just tired, sliced most of it
away but left their living mesh untorn.
A furrow trickles a yard or so up, then
peters out in the trunk's scabbed bark.
          Parent
and child's a good fit, as is mentor and
protégé, but for me there's only teacher
and all those students I'm free to call mine
until they're not. How often have I lingered,
another drab fixture in their greenest vista
now turning only ever grayer, as they grow
away? And so this lithe tree and its lopped
trellis will always, I already know, preserve
that first sharp flare of recognition, like
a battery hoarding its voltage.

                              Yet consider
the unpausable feed of things seen, all your instants
firehosing by. Consider next the archive
where time compiles, at the speed of your life, a ledger
too entropic to read. Would it be so strange
if, just this once, chance plucked from the flux an image
that illuminated some page illegible
till now? And if corresponding at random
conjures up merely the mirage of a pattern,
should this moment even matter?
                                      Probably it does.
Probably it must. What else could render it
so casual and yet so thick with portent,
like a still-life by Morandi? His was the art
of disposing bottles and flasks, a box perhaps,
not so we won't wonder how plain seeing
could ever snap so apt a frame around feeling,
but so we'll have to.
                        Maybe it's because
coincidence always contrives to leave
its works unsigned, that I've never known myself
to pay it any mind. Yet today I wish
this dishevelled street were hung with nothing else.

What's Not to Like?

Doors, because they close;
books, after they end;
spring, while it explodes;
cash, until it's spent;

chocolate, because chocolate;
mountains, because a view;
in-person, because internet;
wikis, because don't know;

forests, for what they shelter;
ruins, for all they show;
New York, although it alters,
and New York, although it won't;

what if, because why not;
whatever, because I'm lazy;
right now, because too late
for tomorrow, because maybe.

A Visit from the E-Muse

Wow. Looks like someone needs a hug.
Lucky for you I've always gone
for that undead-at-noon affect,
that but-it's-freezing sweat-glaze.
Mimic my insomniac speech-gush
all you like, but you'll *never*
match my scorched-earth aplomb.
Let's spare you a trip to the FAQs:
I awe like a diva with my avatars,
smack a few fanboys around for show
before (lol) upvoting them. I'm as meta
as a fractal node. Gauge my reach
by counting up the screens I cloud
with an ammoniac sheen of rage.

Want in, noob? Launch no threads
that don't exclude, then just
keep subtracting till you belong
nowhere else. If *anything* I post
sounds like your cue to go full
IRL, you've read too many poems
I didn't write. Asking what the memes
mean tags you as far too basic
to follow. Does anyone actually *like*
what they like? You're not doing this right
unless you rig, for every mind
you're mining, a playpen in the slag.

That's it: just keep scrolling through
the troll-spew of comments to discover
your life-score, somewhere south
of loser. Don't *even*, with the facepalm.
Remember our deal: *you* binge on a one-
quadrillionth wedge of bandwidth pie
as if my jonesing for quick hits of clicks
doesn't matter, and *I* curate your uploads
as if they do. Don't I keep your browser
barnacled in ads that contrive to flatter
by hoarding your trivia, like a stalker?

You're welcome. Remember what you said would happen, if you ever caught me livestreaming your bedroom again?
Me neither. Now, refresh that feed.

Confessional

> *Yeah, I hate empathy.*
>   Solmaz Sharif

Friends, I'm having one of those days.
Everything's bad and getting worse.

It's obvious by now that for all the valiant
and selfless striving, most of us won't

change fast enough for it to matter.
The trash, the cars, the meat, the water:

do your part or don't, trust science
or that guy on YouTube, it's the same. Friends,

as a poet I shouldn't be writing this, but
my mood's in no mood to worry about

how it makes me sound. Challenge accepted.
Ask yourselves this: what were you expecting

when you breezed in here past a title
like the one above? Something squalid and personal,

all binges, breakdowns, and performative trauma?
Sorry to disappoint, but in my disclosure

the catastrophes on display are you, not me.
Fact is, friends, I'm ashamed for our species,

and for most of us as individuals too.
I wish it wasn't like that, but it is. *Boom.*

So you can understand why I'm always
coming back here, this bright noplace

where I'm never too proud to remember
kindnesses shown me when I was poor,

or lonely, or foolish, by someone with nothing
to gain. Because here, the rinsed light of morning

never quite fades from the view out over
green quiltwork fields, orchards, a river

sweeping grandly off toward the sea beyond.
And today you came, which makes me glad

because why shouldn't it? It does. It will.
Here I can wish you, I can wish us all, well.

Bequest

Mithridates, he died old.
            Housman

When death and I at last embrace—
tomorrow, or in twenty years—
let this lovely, blighted planet mourn
losses that leave scars. Not mine.
I won't be around to judge your grief
by how swiftly you plug up the gap I leave,
so just pause. Note the hush. Cue
the upbeat anecdotes. And resume.
Besides, few of you will even notice
the moment when this universe
toggles to *without him* from *with*.
The good news? Neither will I. Call it
an Irish farewell. Case closed.
There's one thing, though, you should know.

Someone's going to be the keeper
of my sole relic, this bezoar
(budding in the alimentary canal,
it's something like a human pearl).
Whoever you turn out to be,
it'll surprise you one fine day
at an inquest or a funeral,
in a courtroom or a hospital.
Me? you'll ask. *Yes, you. Please sign.*
Have a nice day. And there, inside
strips of biohazard tape
or a limp manila envelope,
you'll find a purplish, ovoid hunk
of something that feels both rough
and polished, like sandstone scoured
by a long caress of wind and water.

Toss it in your palm to test
its uncanny, iron-dense heft;
don't let its homely appearance
or off-putting provenance

mar the idiosyncratic charm
my x decades went to form.
In the lightless hothouse of my gut,
pulsing glands and bubbling ducts
squirted their enriching secretions
on heirloom lines of hope and grievance.
There, mulched in blood-borne silt, this fruit—
of me, in me, but not me—grew.
Constant basting by my breath
now supples its lustrous sheath,
but once exiled to the caustic light
out here, shrunken, cold, and dried,
it'll look like some weird old stone
I should've just cut out long ago.

And yet, whether foresight, fear, or vanity,
something makes me skip that surgery.
Had this nugget not sopped up
my decades-long ingestion of
ineluctable carcinogens
(plus all those eluctable ones),
I'd have died from seizures or sepsis
long before composing this.
While contaminants proliferate
every instant of every day
throughout the biome that begins
just outside my pore-flecked skin,
my own pollutants coalesced
into this mass you'll soon possess,
where their toxins, locked fast, abide.
So it happens that I've survived.

Someday, you'll wish to split the shell
enamelling its nodal particle:
once it's cracked like a nut, sawn
in two like a marble onion,
or dissolved in acid, you'll expect to find
trauma's kernel, safely fossilized.

Well, bad idea. There's no fang, splinter,
shard or bullet cached in its center
attesting to some primal wound.
Its core is just one grain of sand,
a speck of blond quartz I swallowed
on my first hapless attempt to float
among waves gnawing the shore
of a tainted sea. Though the reek of tar
and iodine made me retch,
all my spasms failed to purge
(as we now know) this jagged granule
from its bed of virgin-pink tissue.
I'd not yet floundered back to land
when my visceral labors began,
unnoticed, unasked, and unwilled.
As I write, they churn on still.

This irony—that what should kill me's
the one thing that will outlive me—
sank in late, but sink it did.
Which is not to say I understood.
What I know is, certain things happen,
then more things, and because of them
molecules of my bitterest minerals
conglobe in tiers of indigo crystal,
encoding there the arcane chemistry
of my immune response to history.

Which now, dear legatee, is yours.
Watch it iridesce, as if structures
nested within subtly shifted
in answer to your touch. *That's odd,*
you think, *it reminds me of. . .
of. . .* someone or something. Yes, but
distraction wins again. You leave it
somewhere, a shelf, a drawer, until fate
or chance lures your flighty gaze
back to its poised asymmetries.

Contemplating them, you feel
routine's chafing packstraps unbuckle
and fall away. Now look around.
Some things never change. Some just did.

II

Making It Up: An Elegy

for C.M., 1949-2014

1.
Our poem today comes in the form of a story.
But not just any story. An *American* one.
The difference? You'll see.
That's what our poem is for.
The *plot* is based on an incident from some years ago.
It was in the news, though you probably wouldn't remember.
That's because American stories tell only of matters *widely known* and *immediately forgotten.*
In fact, we could describe America as a nation fleeing its past with such unballasted velocity that events barely register as they flit by.
This might also explain the widespread American disregard for poetry, since poems are all about lingering and brooding, a willful refusal to move on.
But that's another story.

2.
We begin with a family.
There's a father and a mother, a daughter and a son.
Nice family. White family.
There's a house. We'll come back to the house.
There's a dog. There's Jesus, of course. There's been a divorce or two.
There's a gun, our first hint this story's the American kind.
There are witnesses. There are neighbors who suspect nothing.
Near its close, there's a suspenseful moment when achieving full-on American storyhood is briefly in question.
But by then *the range of potential endings* has narrowed to just one, which arrives in a *blaze of inevitability.*
Afterwards the dog gets put to sleep.
The house gets torn down.

3.
The *hero* of any American story is officially America, of course, but times have changed.
Whole stanzas of its founding myth, once merely false, now seem defunct.

Certainly within our poem they are.
Hence there's nothing to deflect us from confronting its true hero: *anger, like a cancer.*
Unconventional, but more common than you'd think.
For the father's anger is what makes a scary clown smile.
The mother's anger is the best friend she likes all the more because no one else does.
The daughter's anger duplicates the mother's so closely that they repel each other like magnets.
But the mother dies before this can become an American story, so her anger is now just a lingering caustic fume.
As for the son, he sees no difference between being angry and being right.
Yet to metastasize like this through one brittle family is not enough. Heroes must be seen to act.
And if there's one thing a hero knows to do, it's embark on a quest.
    A quest for what? For whatever can *consummate the heroic potential.*
Our poem agrees, though with a shrug of ironic surrender.
Ironic, since powerlessness before an American story, as if before some unfathomable mechanism or amoral force of nature, is illusory.
Such stories are in truth the result of choices: open and secret, recent and long ago, personal and collective. Artifacts, each with its history.
And reality, the term for today's obvious truths, is the camouflage they wear.
But within our poem, we're free to see and feel otherwise, like characters on whom *the narrative logic* has temporarily lost its purchase.
Because here, true patterns dissolve false ones.

4.
Every story must *traverse an arc.* Poems too, in their way.
But for sundry historical reasons, an American story's arc must spring *from an act of dispossession,* climax in *murderous spectacle,* and terminate in a *consensus of uneasy complicity.*
This occurs on scales ranging from the continental all the way down to the personal.
So it is with this story, where decades of Winstons and Eyewitness News and Korea, of inflamed grievance and eroding privilege, have given the father health trouble.
Which, in an American story, can only mean money trouble.
And money trouble means house trouble.

Bringing us, as promised, to the house.
Here we find the daughter, chronically un- or under-employed, living and
 caring for the father.
She is growing old herself now, and hopes to inherit her home.
But the father knows he's going to live forever and so, as he has all his life, he
 declines to envision the world without him.
Perhaps he'll sell the house, or rent it out. The daughter will just have to move.
Meanwhile, she'll need to get rid of that fucking dog, which he can't stand
 even though it carries his name.
Because the dog, as the only available receptacle for the daughter's intense
 upwellings of affection, snaps at everyone not her.
Such are the small poignancies with which poetry arrests its readers' notice, in
 a space sufficiently private for our impulses of solidarity to fear no
 derision.
Perhaps, even, for our compassion to bloom.

5.
The *setting* for every American story is, naturally, *the lost paradise of male
 nostalgia*.
But this, though true enough, is too abstract for our poem to imagine.
And if there is anything these disjointed and sinister times call for, it is the
 imagination's strobing pulses of instantaneous, all-over clarity, whose
 residue of humane insight persists like an after-image.
The present section of our poem is set by design, therefore, against a black-
 and-white horizon of stark mesas, distant smoke plumes, and grimly
 ripening vengeance.
It is a desolation only the father can see, but which the family are all
 compelled to inhabit.
For it is from somewhere deep within those stony vistas that one Saturday
 morning the father dials 911.
He gives his name and address to the dispatcher.
Then he says, "I just shot my daughter and my dog."
Police arrive. They find it so.
Suddenly the father emerges from a bedroom with a shotgun, which he is
 ordered to drop.
He fails to comply. They kill him.
The daughter is found dying on the kitchen floor. She has been shot once in
 the head.

The dog is wounded, but survives. For now.
In the abrupt desert twilight, enormous shadows unclench and flood across
    the jagged landscape.

6.
If an American story had a *moral*, it would be *aftermath's a bitch.*
But because morals, once drawn, might constrain the appetite for orgiastic
    carnage in subsequent American stories, they are generally
    discouraged.
Oddly enough, poetry shuns them as well but for the opposite reason: a clear
    moral curtails a poem's promiscuity of meaning, thereby licensing
    other poems to ignore it.
And so in both cases, *the denouement* should be a moment fraught with
    ambiguity.
Over time, such ambiguities will only be amplified by memory, whose
    function is creative rather than archival.
Which implies that all memories must ultimately inhere, for better or worse,
    in the individual, whom we can therefore term without grandiosity
    their *creator.*
The son, though he lives in the same city, does not learn what has happened
    until days later.
He has not spoken with the daughter or the father for many years.
He does not attend the funerals or services, if there are any.
The authorities never contact him.
He is familiar with stereotypes of despair like *suicide by cop* and *family
    annihilator,* just as he is aware of many other social ills that deserve
    attending to.
But for him, an American story means the kind of ordeal that occurs
    elsewhere and to other people.
To other *kinds* of people.
Which turns out to be true in a way, since after years of avoiding this, his own
    personal American story, he discovers that he's been exactly that kind
    of person all along.
The *other* kind. Which turns out to be the *only* kind.
Furthermore, by framing his own story as something utterly different from an
    American one, he has become *an unreliable narrator.*
How successfully he has misled others is unclear. Certainly he has deceived
    himself profoundly, in the way that self-inflicted wounds are the most

crippling.
All this comes as no surprise whatsoever to our poem, since poetry is a traditional venue for self-discovery of every kind.

7.
And so.
Life goes on, which is what it does. What it cannot help doing.
The America glimpsed in this American story also goes on, reaching new peaks of improbable grotesquerie with each passing day. So too the sense that things simply can't continue like this, source of the genre's power to enrage, disgust, and horrify.
All three at once, again and again.
Poetry goes on as well, never for a moment permitted to forget how, as a mode of expression hopelessly opaque, elitist, outdated, useless, or self-indulgent, its days are numbered.
Indeed they are, but it is a very high number.
Says the poet.
As regards the family, with three of its four members dead, it hardly exists anymore except through the memory of its sole surviving member.
For the son regularly revisits what happened in his absence.
Perhaps even *because* of his absence.
But it is here, at the foot of *the falling action*, we must leave him.
Because once an American story has visited guilt and sorrow upon the bereaved, while delivering no redemptive insights whatsoever, it reaches its prescribed conclusion.
At the same time our poem, having in contrast spent itself reacquainting us with our own freedom, nears its end as well.
No doubt that white expanse approaching from below comes as a relief to us all.
And finally, this hovering sense of promises kept, of expectations fulfilled, is the sensation known as *closure*.
Always elusive, often quite brief, and on occasion counterfeit, it is nevertheless uniquely satisfying.
So go ahead. Enjoy it.

III

Off into the Sunset

There I go, sauntering along
as if I don't notice
this bright amber evening already
auditioning for your memory,
though naturally I do.
You can tell I'm savoring how
this magic-hour sunlight
ignites tiny tiaras atop the upper edges
of each sombre object I pass
(car, stopsign, mailbox, car, wall),
like a swarm of small dawns I'll remember
to describe for you later—
meaning now—
as a *sizzlation*,
but not just yet.
I'm still basking in the facets
that gleam where bark and steel and brick
are flecked with a luster that will linger
just an instant longer,
the better to arrest them
thus. Besides,
it looks like your mind—
your lovely, captious, queasy mind—is content
to bask in these surfaces too, as if
the world's tide of misery
has receded somewhere far beyond earshot,
exposing this block's homely treasures
for us to admire with the just-
barely-not-ironic gusto
we share like a tic.
It can't last; it doesn't.
A sawtooth skyline steps in front of the sun,
some streetlamps blip on,
and the low-angled light
that'd made even the East River look good
for a moment,
departs. As do I.
You're plugging yourself back in,
and by the time you surface

from the cyan screenglow of your pent-up phone,
there's nothing left to forget
but the moment I turn the corner
into everything that happens next.

East River Suite

> *Cold dark deep and absolutely clear,*
> *element bearable to no mortal[...]*
>   Elizabeth Bishop

1.
With one glance up
at the splintered waters knitting shut
just above my head,
I conclude that Ms Bishop—
my beloved poet
of precision, color, and limit—
was misinformed.

2.
Atop the high embankment, I'd imagined
no danger
from a river of skylines floating
over occulted currents, supposedly the border
between knowledge of the world
and the world.

A parapet proclaimed that here
only the wanton contrive to fall,
and fallen I most haplessly had.
Allure of the brink and all, but still.
Disgrace waited while I gasped
for air.

As I flailed and sank and thrashed and rose,
panic nudged me: *hey, you're almost*
drowned.
Even so, a nip of regret
as I shed the deadweight of new shoes and jacket
dragging me down.

Yet all the while,
a prim report was being compiled
in the one staffed and able bureau of my mind

on how, by whom, and why
I'd been so scandalously
misled.

3.
Cold? Well, every inch of me not
scalded is going numb, so call that
a 'yes.' *Dark*? Check: whether closed
or open, these eyes are proving good
for nothing. *Deep*? Yup: every time
I whipkick my feet for the bottom,
they slice a void. But *absolutely clear*?
Nope. Not down here. Out in the air,
even a noontide sun couldn't drill
enough of itself through this swirl
of umber-tinted silt, to disclose
whatever a clenched hand might hold,
though held just an arm's-length in.
Oh I'll write it, I swore, *if I live*.

4.
I lived.
        *Dear Ms Bishop: first off, it's OK.
Really. Those waters, streaming or standing
within the ideal vistas your stanzas frame,
still reflect the Canada you saw as a child
does, undefendedly. Shimmering, they lie
in the smooth and shadowless light
of memory, their discrete prismatic hues
undimmed for you amid the ragged mists
and rumpled emerald distances
of the Brazil you adored, then lost.
I get it now. It should've been clear
to me why the harsh, astringent tang
you've given those waves, their sullen,
rolling menace glazed with an old-
silver luster, are all to be feared*

only from land. An ocean's its waters,
and you aligned Nova Scotia's with words
lucid as truth should be. Any death they bore,
however dreadful, would come as a surfeit
of something pure.
                         But where I stand today—
yards from the highway, by a tidal cove
whose rust-streaked sands are crunchy with jade
bottle-glass and chunks of plastic debris—
no such threats rumble from these wave-
lets. Instead, they murmur a promise
(still mine to claim) only of further kisses,
each one lavish in the same contaminants
that might, even as I type, be sprouting
some gristly thing from a darkness so deep
inside me, that its first encounter with daylight
will be my last. All because, once a poem ends,
its charms can never seem as real as the sum
of the consequences of yielding to them. Or so,
scanning the opaque seaward flow, I believe.

5.
After heaving me up and out, the EMTs
warned of exposure
to toxins like mercury and lead, PCBs

and sewage, so I threw out everything I'd worn,
scoured my skin, decided
to decide to change. Yet I knew all along

there'd be no purging the knowledge my pores
had dilated themselves
so trustingly for. And now, with sunset raking the harbor,

reflected towers beckon from gold-brocaded waves
till they blur, one by one,
in the ragged murk of a ferry's slow, severing wake.

Poem about Love (Not a Love Poem)

*The best way to hold on to something is to pay no
attention to it. The things you love too much perish.*
                    Shostakovich

Around here, I never know how much I'll care
when the next thing fails, or goes missing, or just ends.
For example, along the avenue I walk every day
I don't always notice that for every tree
there are far more ex-trees: thick amputated columns,
or stubby little stumps, or scraped plots of dirt
the color of cement, or squares of actual cement
where someone just said *OK, enough with this.*
They pass like boxes checked on some medical form.
So many? That can't be good.

There's a way I go sometimes, not often, a sidestreet
I'd almost say I loved, if asked to name my favorite street,
though only children ask such questions and I don't have any.
And to admit it's because of some tree, well, you can imagine
how that'd go. Still, it *is* why: one tall silver maple,
the grain of whose pewtery bark records how the trunk
arched away from the buildings and flexed up, out,
and over the street, reaching for light and space.
Its posture reminds me every time of Michelangelo's Libyan Sybil,
though a quick image search shows no resemblance
beyond an excuse to remember a place where I once was happy.

Which brings me to Shostakovich. His advice,
like most good advice, is inarguably true
and impossible to follow. Because I know
how one desolating day I'll finally come upon that tree
freshly cut down, do I avoid this block, start the farewell now? No,
I just forget about it, like I forget everything except
the next thing I need to do and maybe the thing after that, and walk
anyhow, and go on finding myself there, low orange sun behind me,
the non-sybil still not cut down. Time again to wonder if I so love
Rome only because I can't live there, and what love for his children
did to Shostakovich during the Great Terror, and how much
it has cost me to survive the violent love that is the opposite

of both pretended neglect and real neglect,
and when, at long last, our Earth will have had enough
of whatever it is—call it love—that goes on cutting down more
and more of the trees it didn't even plant, along with those it did.

By Sapphire Pool, Yellowstone

> *A large clear blue pool, Sapphire [...] has an average temperature of 158ºF (71ºC).*
> National Park Service

A sluggish train of bubbles
comes wobbling up
like blobs of molten glass,
gooey and hot.

I can't tell yet whether
it's the scale of Wyoming,
or these gigabytes of nature
we've been posting,

or just the estranging effect
of mumbling "sapphire,"
that brackets off this moment.
Soon nothing will matter

but the steam, proof that this color,
though frigid and forbidding,
in fact belongs to waters
noiselessly simmering.

Because now it's all about purity:
the peculiar shock
of a transparence so absolutely
beyond us to blot.

A Brief Loss of Momentum

      I somehow seem to be leaving my apart-
ment late a lot these days, in fact pretty much
every time. I know it's a bad habit,
but I'm OK with how it vectors me out
into this, the hive-roar of New York City,
plated afresh in that alloy of purpose
my oyster-shy life otherwise lacks.
There'll be no swerves. No no-you-firsts.
None of the idle noticing that makes the tug
of analog vistas such a nuisance.
If it's raining, as it is tonight, I'll let
the onyx prongs of Manhattan's overworld
outmenace the first *Blade Runner*'s LA
all they want, so long as my trajectory can arc
through its boulevards' arterial spurt and throb
undeflectably. Like I said, a bad habit.

      So now, with ant-black traffic slithering up Third,
a sift of pinpoint drizzle diffracts
lunar haloes from streetlamps, my cue to note
the contours of every hard thing diluted and blurred.
As my privileged pace sputters out, I must register
first that old woman with a walker hurrying
slowly across the avenue, who gets almost
halfway before the red hand starts flashing,
then this homeless man, no coat, no hat,
no *shoes*, who's shaking a crumpled cup
at a river of umbrellas plunging past.
I'm shunted aside while I peer around,
wondering if I really care to know
how much of this might be other than this
were I not of what keeps it so.
Which is what I get for slowing down.

A Long Walk on an Empty Beach

The sea that is always counting.
                Christopher Logue

You've got to respect it, how the cormorants at first
pretend not to notice us,
each one perched atop
its pole, every dark-crested head now
swivelling
as we approach, until,
out of subtly tensing postures
and a rippling flock-wide flutter,
they vault as one into flight, skimming
over wind-crisped cobalt water,
west over the bay, east over the sea, away from nothing
but us—

And so what, if there's only some mirage of a project
to stoop us down into our cool indigo shadows,
scrabbling for shells that quote the sun, gold-
flecked, gold-spritzed, gold-lacquer-
dipped, which,
chinkling for now in your pocket,
will be bundled home, short-, then long-listed, perused
the once,
then bottom-drawed, unthought-of, cracked, lost,
trashed—

No regrets either when, in exchange
for dawdling along the braid of tidewrack
two whole miles farther,
we find that its fossil-white driftwood, pecked-over
crab carapaces, and scribbles of kelp
not only have nothing new to offer,
but cost us that much more late-afternoon sun
hard on our faces for the walk
back, now that we're walking back, since there's no other way
but back—

Because what's left for us at last,
after retracing our paths
out onto the tidal flats,
and sloshing ahead some more
through the onward gush of the current,
then just wading on past
while the prints of people, birds, a dog,
blur under one swipe from a wavelet
after another,

is to acquire,
as a tempo fit for our own occurring,
this fluent local rhythm
of, for quite some time now,
nothing mattering.

On Being Deciduous

Nothing like a storm
to blazon the wisdom
of wintering trees
that jettison their leaves.

Scrapping the glory
of an emerald canopy
lets them resist
wind-lash less:

not much can snag
on a skeletal twig.
The lushly-attached
get their branches snapped.

They collude with loss
to claim, as their choice
from the catalog of griefs,
one spring relieves.

Víti, a Volcanic Lake in Iceland

Charcoal uplands, barren and crumpled.
Lunar distances, a serrated horizon,
low murky skies. Rain this morning.
Rain again soon.

A puddled uphill path, slimy
with trodden ochre mud, skirting
the pipes and outbuildings of a hydrothermal plant,
sleek and toylike and alien
against this jagged umber sea
of scabbed-over lava.

At the top of the rise, more mud
slickening the approach to the unfenced rim
of a fissured escarpment.
Down where the crater
plunges like a puncture,
our first glimpse of what we came for:
a pool,
blown-glass smooth, improbably blue,
and aglow like a sapphire ember
stoked by breaths from a sun
slathers of cloud keep hidden.

We look and look,
but discover nothing
dyed that unlikely color
for these waters to mirror.

And so,
almost dissuaded from fancying ourselves
as likewise bedded, jewel-bright,
amid broken tracts of circumstance
but not quite,

we turn away as one
into the weather coming swiftly on.

Black Beach Idyll

Late afternoon. Subarctic shoreline.
Sun nowhere to be seen.
Beneath an opaque white sky
rolls an opaque gray sea.

Look: a jumble of purpleorange, buoyant
on the cinder-colored shingle,
enfolds the exuberant PDA
of a bubble-jacketed couple.

They frolic and spoon in a trough of pebbles
that glisten like droplets of tar.
They've noted the portents—birdless silence,
the punishment that passes for weather,

outcrops of washed-up whale vertebrae—
but keep their anguish on standby.
Ambient daylight had warmed up the gravel
as if in welcome, so they,

too long deprived of uncomplicated joy
to pass it up, lapped it up. Entwined
and nuzzling, they drift sweetly for hours
near where a glacier died.

But how? Easy: just as nothing shows
water's splendor like a water-
fall, so their bliss in shared oblivion
crests here, at the brink of the future.

Autumn Exit

Even here, along
an avenue as dementedly luxe as Fifth,
the sheer aplomb
of late-November ruthlessness
gets itself noticed.

The brittle discards
of iron-black trees
skitter ahead toward the gutters.

Cold pavement feels harder.
Evening reclaims its dominion earlier
and earlier.
An ordeal is underway,
though no one calls it that.

By its marauding, the wind
means nothing,
except how the license of summer
is absolutely over.

Yet it wasn't so long ago, that last spree
of open-toed sauntering
and the sampling of zesty streetfoods.

How sweetly outlandish,
those pastimes of the pastel seasons,
archived now for this looming stretch
of hunkering down,
soldiering on,
and being acclimated to things
being gone.

The View from Land's End

"Mene, mene, tekel..."

We came for the beach—what else?
Bright black pebbles, glazed
over and over for us
by breakers whose corrugated jade,
soupy with algae,
we've sunglassed to gray.
Rubbery kelp-wrack pops and squeaks
beneath our cleated bootsoles.
Seabirds swarm and skim, as if auditioning
for a turn as my next screen saver.
After you get this panorama
captured, cropped, and captioned,
what's there to stay for?
Then as one we clock
a high, windswept, west-facing bluff,
slung from the cliffs like a poolside balcony
primped for its billionth selfie.
What with FOMO kicking in,
no way we're skipping
those dolphin-porn backdrops you only get
where some plus-size landmass,
zebra-striped with timezones,
tapers to a drop-off so abrupt
it gets itself dubbed
"Finisterre."
So we head up there.

*   *   *

During the usual half-assed uphill scramble,
we shed any sense
of the ocean's embrace
until, brought up short
by the grass-hemmed, path's-end brink,
our post-brunch spree turns epic.
At this height, the screech of the waves
that emery away
the headlands beneath us
can't reach us. Besides,

these days we *own* the role
of feckless disaster tourists
—red-eye reduced, of course. And now,
teetering blithely on the Old World's fractured edge
while aiming our backs at the New,
we grin to register
the utter fucked-up-ness
of anyone grinning from, of all places,
here.
Meanwhile, the North Atlantic horizons us
—or would, were
its distances not,
like its future, lost
in the kind of colorless curtaining mist
we exhale, or would, in the winter temperatures
we dressed for
but never got.
Still, somewhere out there
the vast azure-fissured ice-sheets of Greenland
are emptying their pre-Anthropocenic waters
into this very sea,
which fills up slowly enough
to make an hourglass's bottom bulb
must-watch TV.
And which has also, by escalating our risk
of having to care about this,
cued us to leave.
* * *

Two steps and we're stopped.
Down there, low over the dunelands,
a chevron-shaped blur
grows brighter, larger, nearer:
a lone Arctic Gull,
uncompromisingly white
against dimming newsprint skies.
Something in the fact
its wings don't flap,
something about how
it zeroes in slow . . .

Swooping so close
that even my short sight can lock
on the crimson-tipped beak,
it banks slightly
to circle us slowly,
shoulder-high
and unhurried as a shark.
Tracking its onside eye, a black
unblinking bead,
the two of us
pivot once around the compass,
then watch its outspread wingtips fade
back inside the sepia landward haze.
Well now.
Just what the hell *that* was
we both wonder,
while knowing better
than to ask so much of the other
as now to,
for the actual, out-loud, all-is-lost answer,
actually ask.
So we get in the car and drive away,
without a word
and fast.

NaCl

> *You know*
> *what despair is; then*
> *winter should have meaning for you.*
>   Louise Glück

Come dawn, nightfallen snow muffles New York.
Nothing looks hard under blue-white fur, but it will.
Shovels start scraping wet felt off our sidewalk
even before the last bedraggled flakes can fall.
Tires churn fleece to slop. Snowblowers snarl on.
And the salt—five boros' worth—cascades by the ton.

The coarse white crystals Rome's legionaries sowed
along furrows gouged through a razed capital's ash;
minerals that leach, keeping the Dead Sea dead;
a caustic grit to sprinkle on whip-latticed flesh:
all sour the dust we'll be tracking inside for weeks
once the city's dumptruck convoys cropdust our streets.

On a printless stretch of pavement, chunks of rocksalt
burn like cinders through a slack skin of slush.
They splatter the snow with lesions of exposed cement
like the voids that riddle the moon's darkside crust.
Look close: bull's-eye in every dilating crater
a single granule basks, poised as a spider.

Nothing to spike a snow-day like saline vomit.
Aged five, I once retched up hot brine for hours,
learning how we kill off ice with pellets of halite
and not, ever, the nonpareil's beadlets of sugar.
Appearances can deceive: sad but true.
Yet salt's still my favorite as condiments go.

Time for us locals to go about our business
in this glittering, glassed-in termite colony.
Meanwhile, runoff sluices through miles of sewers
to empty where life, they say, began: the sea
our forest-primeval forebears knew no better
than to venerate, like earth, like night, as their mother.

All or Nothing/Nothing at All

every song an elegy
every laugh a gasp
every virgin future
a vector of its past

every redline rearviewed
get over it already
every blue-green habitat
dying dead or deadly

never mind the melting
someday it'll stop
nowhere not a dumpsite
no one's mopping up

no need to buy organic
no more sorting the trash
no sad face for the die-offs
not long now to aftermath

IV

Another CNN-Induced Lyric Outburst

"—Bad news first thing
this morning, the whole day's ruined,
it's over, but hold on now, let's show
some initiative here, why settle *again*
for being a defeated observer of the spectacle
when I am, after all, a creator, in fact
a poet, and so it falls to such as me to align
the channels of language with the floods of feeling,
such as they are, let loose by these times,
such as *they* are, yet not through a poem
about the bad news, because
it's not *about* the bad news (it's about
what we *do* about the bad news, right?), no,
but instead with a poem—which, to review,
is a verbal artifact widely considered
forbiddingly esoteric but actually,
if done right, a source of unique
and lasting pleasure—a poem that betrays
a love of its world (which of course includes
the bad news), and seems to know much more
than it has room to say, and seduces us by design
into almost remembering it, a poem that knows better
than merely to distract from the bad news,
or enact a generic outrage over it, or brandish
whatever gestures are popular right now, or even,
as I think does happen, aestheticize the bad news
and thereby collude in it, so *no*, not
a poem like that, but one that does for the reader
what the Earth does for its forests, what
the forests do for our air, what the dead
end up doing for the living, what the living do
or should do for each other, what each of us is doing
(whether we know it or not) for the future,
what the future, or what used to be the future
(and not the one the bad news just brought closer),
what the future, if we weren't afraid to remember it,
was supposed to do, and might still do, for us all."

"I Did It Because I Am Free"

*to the memory of the Charleston Nine,
and for my country*

1. Someday

The museum visitors glance, nod, and pass along.
A couple trades the crinkle-browed look that means
What were they *thinking*? as they make for the café,
tourists pose for selfies, while to schoolchildren,
already certain ancient history makes *no sense*,

here's even more proof. For under this glass
lies tacked the limp and tattered banner
of those war-besotted, chattel-holding plantocrats
and their stillborn neofeudal pirate-state.
Such emblems, it's explained, would later be raised

like bullwhips brandished to suppress
imagined menaces to an imaginary race,
back when that was still a thing. This specimen
once cracked over Columbia's statehouse grounds
till the day a daughter of those chattels ripped it down.

2. *Ten days before*

One hundred miles away, in Mother Emanuel Church,
Wednesday's bible-study circle interrupts a prayer
to welcome a white man with dungeon-inmate eyes.
He will later recall how their kindness is such
that he almost falters on the threshhold of slaughter

but does not. We lose nine more: Clementa Pinckney,
Myra Thompson, Daniel Simmons, Ethel Lee Lance,
DePayne Middleton-Doctor, Sharonda Coleman-Singleton,
Tywanza Sanders, Cynthia Hurd, and Susie Jackson.
As our President sings, the status quo stands ready.

3. *That day*

But she, as heroes will, has a different idea.
The funerals are almost done. Like a tide, attention
is ebbing, because if it didn't something might get done.
Yet before this aftermath can succumb to an overture
of sirens swarming the usual follow-on massacre,

she's aloft, vaulting impossibly up the pole; into her hand
the stars and bars yield, impossibly tame; out of the scrum
of leather and insignia frothing far beneath her feet,
impossibly, not a bullet reaches to snatch her earthward.
She descends; braves the law; survives arrest. And soon,

for all the twangs of *Dixie* dinning in their ears
and the Lost Cause's coffle clamped to their shoulders,
massa's white children dare trespass on massa's myth
enough to desacralize that scrap of cloth,
though no further. It's a triumph. It's not enough.

4. *Today*

Yet what likelier hope is there, of lessening the distance
that stretches from justice for some to injustice for none,
than such fearless virtuosos of creative defiance
as Bree Newsome Bass? "This flag," she said,
"comes down today." And finally, *finally*, it did.

White Lies

Close the book
and shake your head:
makes you think,
what those men did.
Well, days like that are done.
[*number one*]

We arrive to find
no one around.
Once the wars
make it all ours,
we save a lucky few.
[*number two*]

They came here in chains
but we set them free,
[*which makes three*]
so we're not to blame
for what happened before
we were born. [*and four*]

Soldiers we send
to far-off lands
bring freedom's gift.
[*that's a fifth*]
It can't be an empire if
it's us. [*and sixth*]

This country's built
for men who can sprint
ahead of all others,
not for losers
whining the lanes aren't even.
[*and now seven*]

One faith to shape
this nation, [*eight*]
one god to guide
its progress, [*nine*]
one book spelling out when
it ends. [*and ten*]

Sound Effect

Spring, 2020

Come the dawn, clean through
my usual downstream drift
of random, qualm-suppressive
dreaming, there cuts a, not sound,
but sound's hind-edge lull.
Stranger still, to be found
awake where the walls that make
for a house dissolve like doubt,
and all there is is our street's,
bound in grief and not shamed
by its pain. Before this room's accum-
ulations can again occlude
my gaze, I'm heading where, bare,
wrongs too embedded not to wring
their truth from song after song
prove how leadenly they'll linger:
like granules in the tissues, but longer.

A day still loyal to its night.
White noise resumes while what illumines
dims. That, thus, seems that. Or
does it? Before fluming off
where next means same, let's name
every hope this reveille hypes.
Let's reclaim *we will* from *you shouldn't*,
can from *could've but couldn't*.
Let's not wind up ended up
still deadended here. Declare
that we're hearing rusty hasps
wrested off, and I'll laugh, *Yeah*.
For those wondering whether or no
what needed breaking in fact
got broke, my take on it is
we should just make sure it did.

But as for you who long to hear
only the fist-eyed grunt
of a tightening grip, I won't
cheer or chide such fear.

An hour ached-for as ours
blazes too briefly to waste
on a case as lost, a cause
as disgraced, as now is,
at long, long last, yours.

Field-Notes from Monster Season

> *[. . .] for the bane and the enlightening of men.*
> Albert Camus

The first proof of the monster's presence
comes as static in your language.
Trying to speak its name, people say instead
Master, or *Other. Error. Better.*
Bastard. Whatever.

TV knows everything about the monster
except how to stop it.
It's coming for you, and you, and you,
grim panelists warn.
The time to run is now. Then a commercial
for the monster.

Schoolchildren come home crying
when they aren't picked
for Team Monster.

As things escalate,
then escalate some more,
you try to smother your spiking anxieties
with late-night sprees of click-and-swipe research.
A deformed creature, often man-made,
that enjoys inflicting pain and terror on its victims,
destroys what it can, defiles what it cannot,
and remains exquisitely and unseverably attuned
to the imagination(s) that nourished it. Indeed.
But contempt ruptures your solidarity
with those who'd rather suffer the ravages
of a capricious monster
than listen to one more well-intentioned word
from the likes of you.

The advice easiest to remember
may or may not be useful.
When you think the Monster is far away,

behave as if it were present.
Should it close in on you,
just act like nothing's there.

Some nights you awaken to what,
oh god not again,
can only be the shrieks of another victim.
Yet by morning all is normal.
What monster? the neighbors ask
who seem happy, or at least OK.
You want to be happy, or at least OK,
don't you?

On an A-day, the latest monster tidings make you frantic:
rant-hoarsened, all-caps, *can't-possibly-go-on-like-this* frantic.
On a B-day, you can dismiss all the fuss:
This has happened before. It'll be over soon.
With time come C-days, when your brain
hums along monster-free for hours at a stretch.
Whichever one you're having, the others seem impossible.

You want hope.
Is there no hope? you wail to your best friend,
the search engine that respects your privacy.
Scrolling its cascade of inspirational memes,
you wonder if you're better or worse off
finding comfort here.

You cannot understand how the monster
can be wrong about everything,
but always right about you.

Some, aware their right to belong
can be revoked at any moment,
know the ways of monsters well.
From you, the inborn violence of this violent place
has never been hidden.
Now they know what it's like, you think.
Welcome to our world.

But should the word *monster* sound too childish
to utter without irony,
blame your lifetime of exemption and safety.
Accustomed only to fears about entrance exams
or a partner's continued willingness
to keep their infidelities discreet,
yours is the severer shock.
Between the you of today and the child
too frightened to peek from under the blanket,
there stretches a distance that,
however many years long,
the monster covers in one swift horrible spring.

To the expected objects of dread, add
the shame of falling prey.
Didn't listen. Wrong place wrong time.
No common sense. No self-respect. No gun.
These people. Those countries. That religion. This mindset.
The monster's choices now seem inhumanly random,
now intimately regular.
Your fault, if it is a fault, lies
in flitting from the one to the other,
again and again, every day.

Whenever you howl once more
When will this end?
remember that plenty of people don't want it to.
After all, nothing, not even monster season,
is bad for everybody.

Sometimes all it takes is an image on a screen:
hands gripping a chainlink fence,
a scattering of unclaimed shoes,
oily smoke pluming over a landscape.
Or a human, maybe old, maybe young,
in a tent, on a line, atop a gurney,
looking to you.

So much suffering,
you hear in the sudden inner hush,
so, so much.

As for your vision of the impending
year-zero reckoning,
let your zeal for a purge
of holed-up henchmen and scurrying lackeys
console you, untroubled
by history's noncommittal shrug.
Even a mirage of justice
is better than its opposite
for our survival.

Scrolling through Weimar

Gray vets glower in vain
at foppish youths who laugh
as another dynastic bronze
is trundled off for scrap,

and cabaret divas affecting
an exquisitely decadent calm
layer cooings of impunity
over simpers of smothered alarm,

and matrons cheer on hooligans
to spike the heads of scholars
who offend by outing providence
as a botch of befores and afters,

and motorcades to moated enclaves
hiss along hosed-off streets
after frontier-toughened troopers
scythe marchers down like weeds,

and screens concenter millions
on wideshots of joyous clapping
for a spotlit figure,
                            nodding as if
he knows what's going to happen.

Staying Sharp

> *Naught can deform the Human race*
> *Like to the Armour's iron brace.*
> William Blake

The damage is always there:
whether caked in forgetting or,
as now, stark from the stripping
an imagined origin brings.

As when bark, rough and fibrous,
scabs over growth rings
whose even intervals of tissue
must narrow and warp till they fuse,
tracing where a steel shank,
its haft broken off, has sunk
like a dead cutting grafted
for the trunk's life; and beyond.

Bayonet, hatchet, or spear—
one chip off the workbench of war—
has dealt so reverberant a stroke
the pith still thrums with the shock,
which a raving in the leaves foretells
ends only when the tree is felled.

To ensure the barbs can sever
webbed capillaries no further,
cells down the gash begin,
not to heal, but to clot, harden,
and die into a stiff coat
of self-secreted cement
casing, like a sleeve, the wound
in a numb, unyielding rind
that proves itself far tougher
than the moist enveloping matter.

Fallen, its remains soon crumble
to nothing but a fist-sized fossil.

Eras pass; continents shift;
the nugget of anguish persists
through forest, suburb, jungle,
floodscape and desert, a kernel
assembling, like a hailstone, shell
upon shell upon shell of minerals
into a hulking, rust-flecked boulder,
scoured, then abandoned by its glacier,
shedding itself now flake by flake
into the sand anchoring its bulk,
and ravaged less by weather
than by one unblunted splinter.

From a trough between dune and dune
it juts like a sullen ruin,
where figures blurred by heat—
perhaps like us, perhaps not—
stand gazing upwards, together
in what looks, from afar, like wonder.

Premonitions of Civil War

6 January 2022

So much going on right now
that shouldn't be—

a scruffy rosebush mobbed by bees
in January—

there comes a point where it's no good
looking away—

they always said this would happen
someday—

why pretend you and I share anything
but fear—

can't say we don't see it coming
so yeah—

Terminus

> *The permanent is ebbing*
> Jorie Graham

There were never many trains for us to take
and most are long gone by now.
The big arrivals board is blank. Or broken.
The help desk went dark hours ago.

That scruffy local crosses the decrepit hall
for another quick one at the bar.
He seems amused to find us still here, still spiked
on our droll illusion, departure.

Phone-faced children sprawl like flotsam. Another family
gets escorted off: when you ask why, a uniform shrugs.
The woman feeding the trash pyramided over its bin
pivots away as it gently avalanches.

The newschannel shuffles floodscapes, char, a cataract
of protest. Heart-attack orange splatters
map after map. Arrows knit cartel hierarchies
or evacuation routes. Red carpets fritter.

Either the announcements are garbled, or I've lost my ear
for the beige idioms of official disregard.
Adscreens on endless loop splash an ice-blue glow
that eases our passage from outraged to bored.

Your turn to luggage-sit, mine to scavenge a concourse
of forlorn boutiques. Asking for change, the vet
with no legs offers the eye-contact I can't return.
If it's too late, fuck it, his placard says.

NOTES

Epigraphs: The lines by Brecht are drawn from "To those born later," as published in Poems 1913-1956 ed. Willett and Manheim. Rich's lines can be found in "What Kind of Times Are These," from *Dark Fields of the Republic*.

Synchronicity: Jung gave more than one definition of this term; the formulation cited here is from a lecture he gave in 1951, "Über Synchronizitat," later translated in *Man and Time*, 1957.

Confessional: Sharif is quoted from her interview with David Naimon on *Tin House's* "Between the Covers" podcast series: https://tinhouse.com/podcast/solmaz-sharif-customs/. Accessed 9 Oct 2023.

Bequest: A.E. Housman, *A Shropshire Lad* LXII, "Terence, this is stupid stuff." The word "bezoar" (rhymes with *wheezer*) derives from the Arabic (or Persian) word for "antidote, counter-poison." Well into the modern era, these peculiar objects were thought to have medicinal powers.

Making It Up: An Elegy: The incident at the center of this poem took place on 12 April 2014 in Queens, New York.

East River Suite: Bishop's lines are from "At the Fishhouses."

Poem about Love (Not a Love Poem): Shostakovich's words, which he may well have said, can be found (somewhere) in *Testimony: The Memoirs of Dmitri Shostakovich*, "as related to and edited by" Solomon Volkov.

A Long Walk on an Empty Beach: Logue's line is quoted from the "Pax" section of *War Music*.

Víti, a Volcanic Lake in Iceland: The name of this crater, near Myvatn in the island's north-east, is the Icelandic word for "Hell."

The View from Land's End: The epigraph quotes the Book of Daniel 5:25, the writing on the wall at Belshazzar's Feast: "God hath numbered thy kingdom, and finished it. [...] Thou art weighed in the balances, and art found wanting."

Black Beach Idyll: Okjökull was a glacier in western Iceland. Declared officially defunct in 2014, it was memorialized by a plaque entitled "A Letter to the Future," in 2019.

NaCl: Glück's lines are from "Snowdrop," in her volume *The Wild Iris*.

"I Did It Because I Am Free": The poem opens and closes with the words of Bree Newsome Bass, activist, singer, writer, and filmaker. On 27 June 2015, Ms. Bass scaled a flagpole in front of the South Carolina State House and removed a Confederate battle flag, which flew there as mandated by a 1961 state law. Her act of civil disobedience took place ten days after the Charleston Church Shooting, in which fourteen members of the Emanuel African Methodist Episcopalian Church were shot by a white supremacist, nine of whom died. As she descended, Ms. Bass shouted to the police waiting to arrest her, "You come against me with hatred and oppression and violence. I come against you in the name of God. This flag comes down today." The charges against her and another activist, James Ian Tyson, were later dropped.

Two weeks later, the South Carolina legislature voted to formally remove the Confederate banner, then-Governor Nikki Haley signed the bill into law, and the flag was lowered one last time. For now.

Field-Notes from Monster Season: Camus is quoted from the final paragraph of *The Plague*.

Staying Sharp: Blake's couplet is from "Auguries of Innocence."

Terminus: Epigraph from the title poem of Graham's *Sea Change*.

James McKee and his wife live in Queens, New York, where they both work as high-school educators. A New Yorker by birth (and likely by death), he enjoys failing in his dogged attempts to keep pace with the unrelenting cultural onslaught of late-imperial Manhattan. After studying Philosophy & English in college, he held a number of ludicrously unsuitable jobs before spending over a decade as a teacher and administrator at a small special-needs high school. His poems and essays have appeared sporadically, if widely. *The Stargazers*, his first book-length collection, was published in the otherwise uneventful spring of 2020. He spends his free time, when not writing or reading, traveling less than he would like and brooding more than he can help.

www.ingramcontent.com/pod-product-compliance
Lightning Source LLC
Chambersburg PA
CBHW022017160426
43197CB00007B/466